Healing Hope Workbook

A Thirteen Week Study Companion to

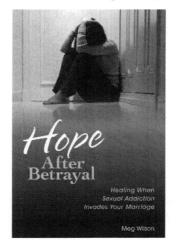

© 2013 Copyright by Meg Wilson

Published by Meg Wilson; printed in the United States of America. All rights reserved. No portion of this book may be reproduced, stored in a retrieval system, or transmitted in any form or by any means — electronic, photocopy, recording, without the prior written permission of the publisher. The only exception is brief quotations in printed reviews.

Library of Congress Cataloging-in-Publication Data Wilson, Meg.
Healing Hope Workbook: Healing When Sexual Addiction Invades Your Marriage / Meg Wilson. p. cm.

ISBN: 978-0-9986862-0-2
Unless otherwise indicated, Scripture is taken from THE MESSAGE Version
™. Copyright by Eugene H. Peterson © 1993, 1994, 1995, 1996, 2000, 2001, 2002. Used by permission of NavPress Publishing Group.
Used by permission. All rights reserved worldwide.

Introduction

Every new class hears me say, "I'm sorry you are here and I'm glad you are here." I'm sorry that sexual addiction is real and must be faced by anyone. My heart also breaks at the resulting pain. I have been there. But I'm glad you are reading these pages and have a resource. I pray you find support through these pages and also from other women ready to study with you. After more than 12 years, it's still a huge privilege to offer hope to others. I assure you, though, the brokenness was not God's choice — He is not limited nor is His plan ruined by what happened.

I understand the doubts. Many women have sat before me and asked, "Why do I have to work, when this was my husband's fault?" If that's you — hang in there. You may not have asked for this path, but God has something for you that has nothing to do with your spouse. This is not your fault nor does it means you are a co-dependent. Your anger is a normal reaction and I pray you use it to push through the healing process.

Regardless of what your husband does or does not do, you can find healing. It is hard work to ask God to shine a light into your heart and reveal what He finds, but this is work worth doing because it pays eternal dividends! God said we would have trouble in this world, but we are not alone and our helper, Christ, has overcome the world.

Step one, is to embrace the process. Lay down any pride that says, "I don't need this." Then sit before the Lord in honesty. That means give Him your anger, resentments, disappointments, any unforgiveness, and pain. Take the first step which says, "This is too big to carry; I need help." Then build on that step. You will get out of this book whatever you put into it. So, do the lessons, even the ones you don't want to do or feel you don't need. Come to each one expecting to hear from God and seeking to learn. You will not be disappointed.

This study is designed to be a companion to the book, Hope After Betrayal. Each lesson is designed to take what was learned in the reading of each chapter and apply the principles to your own life. Additional insights, questions, and practical homework, are designed to move you through the healing process with truth, tools and hope to encourage your journey.

I pray the Holy Spirit leads this process, and reveals the healing power of your Great and Loving Savior to your deeply broken heart.

Class Guidelines

For class time and sharing, it's important to lay some ground rules in order to build trust. Healing takes place in safe communities with mutual respect and vulnerability. (The following was adapted from *"Life Path"* (Salem Alliance Church, used with permission.)

You are Responsible for You

Share using "I" words. We love to help others, but this is not that group. Each woman needs to focus on her own journey. Leave your husband at home. Keep talk about him only as it relates to your work. His healing is not your job. Also, don't compare, because every journey is unique and personal and every person moves at her own pace.

Be Confidential

Its essential that each person feels safe to share. Many have nowhere else to process such a deep and personal betrayal. We share our stories in order to encourage each other. We find we are not alone and healing can begin, but each woman owns her own story and they are not to be taken and shared. Making this commitment to your classmates builds trust. Do not identify anyone from the group to someone outside of the group (even your spouse).

Be Respectful

That means listening more than talking. Please don't give input into others' situations, as this can cause others to feel unsafe. Listening is the greatest gift you can give each other.

Let the group facilitator and the Holy Spirit do the teaching. You are not responsible to help someone else learn.

Be Open and Honest

Accept each person where they are and present yourself as you are. No one is perfect, but if we walk together in truth we can learn from each other. Do not deny, stuff, or run away from your pain or emotions. In order to grow, be open about your fears, doubts, lack of understanding and imperfections. Tears are an important part of healing.

Encourage Others

Seek to build up and encourage each other. Preserve and celebrate achievements, breakthroughs, and *"Ah ha moments,"* both yours and others. Acknowledge the risks and small steps taken when we share in the group. Remember we are all in the same boat and on the same team. Be honest if someone oversteps their bounds. Nothing is wasted if we will let God teach us through even the messy parts.

Do Your Work

Commit to not only the time you meet with others, but also to the time needed to work through the homework. The more time you allow, the more time you have to hear from the Lord, thus the more you gain. Your primary teacher should be the Holy Spirit as you seek God's heart and truth for your situation. Invite Him in prior to reading and writing. Ask for His leading and then expectantly wait. This should not be a "check off the box" kind of study; rather, the questions and exercises are designed to open up dialogue between you and the Lord. Come expectantly!

Journal Regularly

There are lots of journal prompts in *Hope After Betrayal* and more opportunities in this workbook. Journaling is an important part of processing regardless of whether you are creative and draw or cut and paste or write/type pages and pages. This is the time to let your thoughts, feelings, and brain fog flow out into a tangible form. This is a powerful place for the Holy Spirit to work. Even if it feels foreign, try it both in writing and in a creative format such as answer prompts or cut out pictures for a collage. (Appendix A, *HAB*, pg. 153)

I will provide you with the facts about sexual addiction, the healing process, healthy vs. unhealthy behaviors and your role in recovery. I am not a counselor, though I have logged plenty of hours with counselors. Let me encourage you. After having walked this path now with dozens of women, I have seen and experienced the places we get stuck as well as the beauty of God's illumination in those dark places. Watching ladies come in on the verge of tears, broken and without hope makes me all the more resolved to be God's voice in the darkness. It's a joy to say with confidence, if you stick with this material and more importantly, with God, at the end of this class you will leave with your head held high and armed with the truth. Hope will restore the color in your cheeks and you will be clothed in righteousness, ready to go wherever God is calling.

Introduction
Homework

Read pages 11-26 in *Hope After Betrayal*: My Path and Introduction.

Write out your hopes for or feelings about, this class. What would you like to see happen?

_____

_____

_____

_____

Here are some of the words from my journal early on in the process:

Lord, I need Your strength and wisdom because I'm fresh out. It feels like life sucks! Show me how to live in the light of Your truth because I'm easily deceived. I have been hurt so many times. I want to protect my heart. I feel numb, because even when I try to explain my feelings, there is no understanding or empathy, only defensiveness from my husband. I'm so tired of this #$@; (you don't have to *edit out any colorful language because it's for your eyes only. And God already knows.) And I'm too tired even to be angry. Give me new steps, Lord. My hope must be in You, I see that no one else can be my Savior. Everyone else is dealing with their own issues. Help me, Lord, to take one step.*

Now prayerfully write your prayer to Him. Express what you are feeling. Yes, even the hard stuff. He can take it. Write it all out. Then begin to put down in writing what you would like to gain from this study and group if you are in one. Share this part with the group next week or with at least one safe person.

_____

_____

_____

_____

_____

_____

(If you need more room attach a piece of paper.)

In each chapter of *Hope After Betrayal,* I give a few *"Path Lights"* that helped illuminate my way toward healing and wholeness.

What do I mean by the term Path Light? They are specific principles/truths from God's Word that illuminated a concept or aspect of God's character I had not seen before. They were powerful in keeping me in the arena of truth and out of the muddy waters of fear, shame, and pain.

Throughout this workbook, I will encourage you to find your own Path Lights. You can begin with my examples. I will provide some other Scriptures and then as you search those Scriptures, I trust God brings you to places He has for you as He illuminates your personal journey.

Take a look at the first Path Lights on page 25 of *Hope After Betrayal.* Write down the one that jumped off the page or write down another if you already have one in mind.

Write it down to see it, claim it, and re-read it for yourself!

_____

_____

_____

_____

Optional: Take some time to listen to your favorite worship song. Imagine the face of God as you listen. He inhabits the praises of His people *(Psalm 22)*.

Lesson One - Blackout

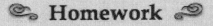 ### Homework

Read Chapter One, pages 27-39 in *Hope After Betrayal.*

The shroud that covers the light and leaves us in darkness is made up of lies. This lesson is about addressing some of the most common misconceptions. My hope is that this tool will be one you continue to use as you take every thought captive *(2 Corinthians 10:5).*

It's the power of a lie to create complete and utter blindness. It is why replacing the lies in our lives with the truth of God's Word is a consistent theme in the book and throughout this study. I believe it is the most life changing process we can commit to. Opening our hearts up to God's power to change will mean the death of many lies and will breathe life into all our relationships. Lies are subtle, they often run deep, and are tied to past pain and poor teaching. They also leave the same kind of pain and destruction in their wake while we go forward unaware. Let's start with three common lies people believe.

Lie #1: Looking at pornography is harmless adult entertainment.

Much of the world feels this way. The media has convinced us by calling those who would disagree "prudes," or "out of touch." We are made to feel backward as just about every form of public expression pushes sexually charged images at us. I can't watch TV, listen to the radio, or go to the mall without being bombarded. Sex sells for sure, but what about the consequences? You may have even bought into the lie that a little porn would spice up your marriage. Your husband may have convinced you. Some of you felt the need to compete without knowing why. Don't beat yourself up, just take another look.

Truth: This *"harmless"* entertainment leads to disrespect, degradation, and abuse toward women and children. Demand for porn also fuels the need for more material and increases the number of victims of sexual crimes and sex trafficking.

Watch TV, then note every time you see sex used to sell or hear a news story dealing with a sexual issue.

_____

_____

_____

_____

Were you surprised by the results or did this exercise confirm your thoughts?

_____

_____

_____

_____

When you see a woman provocatively dressed, what would you like to say to her?

_____

_____

Can you see she too is a victim of lies? (It's okay if you're not there yet.)

Lie #2: My partner's addiction has something to do with me.

Now, I may be getting closer to a dark place most of us find after being betrayed by our most intimate friend. The lie sounds something like this, *"Surely, if I had done something different or looked more like the images and/or person he cheated with, he would not have felt the need to stray."* It FEELS true and even seems to fit some sort of logic. You may have even had someone tell you to be more available sexually to your partner to avoid being betrayed. But this is just as untrue as lie #1.

Truth: There is nothing you did, or could have done, to cause another person's poor choice. I'm pretty certain you did not hold a gun to his head or twist his arm.

After walking with hundreds of amazing women, I can safely say any perceived flaws were not the cause of their partner's choices. Time after time from the mouths of the men, they say they love their wives and hate their choices. Every honest man realizes his behavior has more to do with the insanity of addiction and the need to medicate pain than any flaw of their wife. In all the years of working in this ministry there has never been an exception. Did you fully absorb this truth? You are not to blame! This is not your fault.

What are the lies you hear in your head about why this happened?

_____

_____

_____

_____

_____

What is the one thing you wish you could change about what has happened? Write your answer as a letter to God, be honest and raw.

_____

_____

_____

_____

_____

Lie #3: God has abandoned me. How could He let this happen?

It is not hard to feel like God was not paying attention to allow this kind of pain in your life. I spent some time reminding God of all the ways I had been a good wife, mother, and Christian. Didn't He owe me something based on all my good deeds? It's hard even to type this now, as I see how steeped in lies and misconceptions those early thoughts were, but God listened and even answered my *"Whys."* He will do the same for you, so be honest about how you feel He let you down or left you vulnerable. He can take it. I thought I had dealt with this when, months later, I was having a bad day. I was angry, but didn't know why. My husband quoted our counselor who often said, "If you did know, what would it be?" I took a second to ask myself this question and I heard the answer, ugly as it was. I said, *"I did everything right, and still got screwed!"* There was still residue for me to work through. This is a tough lie to break free of.

Truth: *God assured us, 'I'll never let you down, never walk off and leave you, we can boldly quote, God is there, ready to help; I'm fearless no matter what. Who or what can get to me?* (Hebrews 13:6)

Have you ever felt abandoned? If so, when and who was it?

_____

`
_____

Is there another lie you feel God has shown you this week? If so, what is it?

_____

_____

_____

_____

_____

Find your own *"Path Light"*. Search scripture until God brings you a truth to combat the above lie or a promise He has for you. I trust Him to guide you.

Write your truth down and put it where you can see it. Claim it for yourself each time you read it!

_____

_____

_____

_____

Begin to answer the journal prompts from *Hope After Betrayal* on page 40.

_____

_____

_____

_____

_____

_____

_____

_____

_____

_____

Now write your story to share with your group. Use separate sheets of paper (*try to keep it under 5 written pages*).

This can be a hard week, revisiting the pain, so take some time for yourself after you do this exercise. Get a coloring book, take a walk, or a bath, or get a massage. Do something you enjoy to help you heal. You have been through a trauma and though the wounds are not visible, they are real. You would do whatever the doctor said if you had cancer, so don't miss this important step.

Lesson Two - Shrouded

🍃 Homework 🍃

Read Chapter Two, pages 41-52 in *Hope After Betrayal.*

I looked to the left, then to the right and uncertainty met me. Then I looked back and realized even the past had changed colors. Old memories that once brought joy were now ugly and full of questions like, *"How could he even say those vows?"* or *"Who was he thinking about on that day?"* Then there was the desire to move forward, but the path was fraught with dangers, hairpin turns, and certain disaster. Should I run, retaliate, or just stay put in the dark?

The lies were coming more quickly now. I was vulnerable to anyone who would offer to help me find the way, though not all help is of God. Thankfully, I waited, trusting the Lord would make Himself known. Here were a few more lies that came up.

Lie #4: I am being punished because of my past poor choices.

This lie goes deep for most of us. Few have gotten through life without some poor choices. Because the enemy knows this and the human tendency is toward fairness and personal justice, this seems to make sense. We have all fallen short, missed the mark, and failed. Instead of running into the arms of our Savior, we look for ways to make things right, balance the scales, etc. We forget what brought us into the faith. I thought believing in Christ would make life balanced. I work hard to be good and He gives me eternal life. Ask anyone, *"How do you get to heaven?"* Most will say, in one form or another: *"Good works."* It makes sense, it's how the world works: Good = reward, bad = punishment. So we feel punished by the painful circumstance and connect it to a past *"bad"* deed. This completely erodes, erases, and eradicates the amazing and incomprehensible work of the cross. Thanks to God we don't get what we deserve — for it would be death. Instead, He created a path to life through Christ. This path is individual — each person must decide to walk in it.

Truth: *This is how much God loved the world: He gave His Son, His one and only Son. And this is why: so that no one need be destroyed; by believing in Him, anyone can have a whole and lasting life. God didn't go to all the trouble of sending his Son merely to point an accusing finger, telling the world how bad it was. He came to help, to put the world right again. (John 3:16)*

Read this verse as if it were the first time. You are not being punished, dearest, even the painful consequences of living in a broken world can be filtered and redeemed through God's heart of love.

Does the enemy condemn you? If so, how? Bring it before the Lord where there is no condemnation.

I don't feel condemned but
maybe "prideful"? Like I
don't see my sin as sin
which can be just as
dangerous

Lie #5: I'm the innocent one.

If you had a hard time with the last lie, then the enemy may have gone the other way and convinced you that you're the victim here. After all, "you don't deserve to be treated this way." All this pain is your husband's fault and you didn't do anything to warrant what happened. Here again is a half-truth. While still you are not responsible for your spouse's choices, you are not without responsibility. You can't side step a poor reaction by using another's bad decisions to validate it. Each person has a load to carry and a burden to bear. We are responsible for our choices and reactions before the Lord. He desires that we lay down our right to punish and let His forgiveness flow through us. It may feel comfortable to wrap up in a victim's blanket, but it's hard to get out once you settle there.

Truth: *Since we've compiled this long and sorry record as sinners and proved that we are utterly incapable of living the glorious lives God wills for us, God did it for us. Out of sheer generosity he put us in right standing with himself. A pure gift. He got us out of the mess we're in and restored us to where he always wanted us to be. And he did it by means of Jesus Christ. (Romans 3:23-24)*

Have you put all of your focus on what your husband has done, giving no thoughts to how God is calling you to respond with grace and truth? Write it as a letter to God.

Dear God,

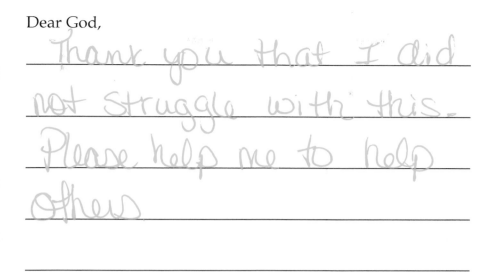

Thank you that I did not struggle with this. Please help me to help others

Lies #6 & 7: Divorce is the only way to end the pain/ divorce is never okay.

I have had so many women quote the Bible to me when it comes to the issue of divorce. These lies are two bookends. Divorce may be the path the Lord has for some women, but it's not a decision to make hastily. Sin is an abomination to the Lord, but He doesn't hate sinners. God offers a perfect balance of grace and truth, we won't find without Him. I could have chosen divorce, I had Biblical justification to stand on, but I chose to listen to the Lord and wait. If my husband chose to stay in his addiction, putting my life and health at risk, I am confident the Lord would have released me from the marriage. You see, God cares about what is happening in the hearts of His kids, not about some paper filed with the courts of men. We must be careful to put our relationship with the Lord above all else, even our marriage.

Truth: *Jesus said, "Moses provided for divorce as a concession to your hard heartedness, but it is not part of God's original plan. I'm holding you to the original plan, and holding you liable for adultery if you divorce your faithful spouse and then marry someone else. I make an exception in cases where the spouse has committed adultery." (Matthew 19:8-9)*

It's clear God's plan is for marriage, but He always offers a contingency for the reality of poor choices. His grace is sufficient for every situation.

Which of the two lies above feels true to you? Write out a list of movies/books/shows that support these lies.

Neither

_____

_____

_____

_____

_____

_____

Find your own *"Path Light"*. Search scripture until God brings you to the promise He has for you. Choose the first verse that resonates. I trust Him to guide you. You may even already have one in mind. Write it down and put it where you can see it. Claim it for yourself each time you read it!

_____

_____

_____

_____

_____

Take special care of *"you"* this week. Treat yourself to something that ministers to your heart. Go to a movie, visit a friend, take a walk somewhere scenic, get your favorite coffee drink, etc. Invite the Lord to come along.

Answer journal prompts on page 52 of *Hope After Betrayal.*

_____

_____

_____

Lesson Three - First Shimmers

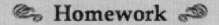 Homework

Read Chapter Three, pages 54-65 in *Hope After Betrayal.*

The first shimmers are the little rays of light which begin to illuminate a new landscape. I pray you are already identifying lies and dark places in your thinking and letting God's light of truth shine in. As you interact in a personal and intimate way with the Lord your relationship soars to new heights.

> *"My sheep recognize my voice. I know them, and they follow me. I give them real and eternal life."* (John 0:28)

I love this picture because there are women who confess they don't hear God's voice. I love to tell them it's not because He isn't speaking; it takes time to learn His voice. We must turn our ear to Him, and begin to listen with faith and expectancy. The first shimmer may just be listening for the Shepherd and learning how He speaks to you. He speaks to some through His Word and some through nature, worship or traditions. Most of us have one predominant language, yet we can learn to see the face of God in many ways.

If you have been walking with the Lord for some time and know His voice, then your first shimmer may be to actively discover your blind spots. A blind spot is a lie we believe is true. Invite the Lord to bring them out. Though the process won't be easy, it will be fruitful. For we all have places too dark to find without help. Discovering God is like buying a new car. Suddenly you see the same make and model everywhere when you never noticed before. Watch with expectancy for God's hand, listen for His voice, He won't disappoint. He is simply waiting for you to ask.

Lie # 8: I don't see God in my situation.

There are times when God feels silent. These are often times to strengthen my faith muscle. When I finally see He was at work in ways I could not have known, I end up asking for forgiveness for not believing; He never leaves or forsakes me. The good news is even when I was impatiently crying out to Him, He was diligently working on my behalf. Over and over I have found God to be faithful even though He isn't always fast! Faith is believing before the evidence arrives to support that belief. I still struggle with this; thankfully, His faithfulness is not dependent upon my faith.

Truth: *Do you think anyone is going to be able to drive a wedge between us and Christ's love for us? There is no way! Not trouble, not hard times, not hatred, not hunger, not homelessness, not bullying threats, not backstabbing, not even the worst sins listed in Scripture. (Romans 8:38)*

Think back to the last time you heard from the Lord or felt His presence. Even if it was when you were first saved, write about how it felt.

Music - Singing in the
Kitchen. With Lori -Peace
Dreams- visions. When I
became sick | vision, Grandma,
Joel, etc

Feelings are not facts, but feelings are real and from the Lord. Be honest with him about your feelings right now. Write out an anger letter to the Lord. I know it's hard to express anger at the Lord, but He can handle it and He sees your whole heart (*add pages as needed*).

_____

_____

_____

_____

_____

This week I ask you to seek His face every day. Ask God to reveal Himself to you in a new, personal and intimate way. Then be expectant. Write what happens.

_____

_____

_____

Read Psalm 116. You are not the first one to cry out to the Lord. Write out your *"case,"* like the Psalmist as a prayer to the Lord.

_____

_____

_____

_____

_____

Read the *"Path Lights"* from *Hope After Betrayal* on page 65 and/or seek your own until God brings you to the promise He has for you. Choose the first verse that resonates. You may already have one in mind. Write it down and put it where you can see it. Claim it for yourself each time you read it!

_____

_____

_____

Answer the journal prompt on the bottom of page 65 of *Hope After Betrayal*.

_____

_____

_____

_____

_____

_____

Lesson Four - Lanterns

✑ Homework ✑

Read Chapter Four, pages 67-76 in *Hope After Betrayal*.

Having heard from the Lord last week, you are ready to begin to let Him lead you to a safe person. It may be a Christian counselor, friend, or support group but as long as the Lord is leading the way you can trust the path. He can speak to us in many ways and one of them is through other people. It's important to move slowly and not share indiscriminately with anyone who will listen. When someone who has walked a similar path shares her experience it is healing for both people. It's one of the ways God redeems our painful experiences.

Notice, most lanterns don't flash or have a harsh light. They simply add a beautiful glow to the area around them. Safe people are like this. They don't demand to know details, they don't attract attention, they simply cast a Godly glow on those close to them. As you pray for a safe person to walk with you, listen to any names that come to mind then proceed with caution.

The enemy would love for you to believe you have no friends.

*Note to wives of pastors/missionaries/ministry leaders:

I know this idea brings another set of challenges. Your husband's loss of position is at stake if you tell the wrong person. Your husband may have given you "spiritual" reasons to remain silent and submissive. If your husband is seeking help, then you should be able to do the same. There are confidential avenues like counseling and online resources. Suffering in silence won't bring glory to the Lord. If your husband has refused to get help, then you must seek confidential guidance. Doing nothing is silently sanctioning his sinful behavior. The losses feel too big but remember the Lord is so much bigger!

Lie #9: Sharing my pain makes me needy. I don't want to burden others.

This is a Western idea stemming from the old "pull yourself up by your own boot straps" mentality. This country was founded by individuals who sought independence and stood for being their own person. There are wonderful aspects to this type of strength. It is only half of the story since the early Americans had to lean on each other and found their strength in community. The label "needy" gets attached to people in church who continually complain about their situation yet refuse to take proactive steps. The truth lies in the middle. We all need the help of our Savior!

Truth: *Responsibility is individual, care is corporate. Make a careful exploration of who you are and the work you have been given, and then sink yourself into that. Don't be impressed with yourself. Don't compare yourself with others. Each of you must take responsibility for doing the creative best you can with your own life. (Galatians 6:4-5)*

Sharing others' burdens isn't carrying them. Stoop down and reach out to those who are oppressed. Share their burdens, and so complete Christ's law. If you think you are too good for that, you are badly deceived. (Galatians 6:3)

Lie #10: Good Christians don't put up boundaries.

It is important to distinguish between a boundary and a wall. The picket fence is a good image as it allows safe people access, while leaving a barrier when someone has proven to be destructive. Putting up walls prevents growth and Godly connections.

Truth: *Healthy boundaries help both parties distinguish where one ends and the other begins. "A person without self-control is like a house with its doors and windows knocked out. (Proverbs 25:28)*

Prayerfully, check at least two boxes. Some healthy places to look for safe people are:

☐ Godly Christian counselor

☐ Friend or leader in your church

☐ Online group *(www.journeytohealingandjoy.com/join-the-community or www.freedomeveryday.org/spouses-of-sex-addicts/index.php)*

☐ Local support group

☐ Spiritual care team *(Based on the book by Earl & Sandy Wilson, and friends, Restoring The Fallen)*

☐ Books and other resources

Write out any fears you may still have about being vulnerable for the Lord. Invite Him to work in these areas.

_____

_____

_____

_____

_____

_____

_____

_____

_____

_____

_____

Write down the ways your family dealt with boundaries, honesty, vulnerability, and failure and if there are any changes you would like to make to these learned patterns.

_____

_____

_____

_____

_____

_____

_____

_____

_____

_____

_____

Write your own *"Path Light"*. Search scripture until God brings you to the promise He has for you. Write it down and put it where you can see it. Claim it for yourself each time you read it!

_____

_____

_____

_____

_____

Answer the journal prompt on the bottom of page 76 in *Hope After Betrayal (compare your answer to the question above about family)*.

_____

_____

_____

_____

_____

Lesson Five - Laser

Homework

Read Chapter Five, pages 78-90 in *Hope After Betrayal*.

It's ironic that I am writing about anger when it's something I struggle with. I admire those women who can speak their mind and be honest about this *"negative"* emotion. Of course that is my bias showing. There are also women who admire those who can hold their tongue and not get swept away in a sea of rage. It's about balance. God created anger, so of course it has its place. I have seen how women who deal well with this emotion are better able to push through their pain, set boundaries, and heal. So as uncomfortable as this lesson may be, it's worth doing well.

Describe what your anger tends to look like.

_____

_____

_____

_____

_____

_____

Lie #11: Anger is not *Christian*.

This is a common misconception in the church. Somehow Christ gets relegated to a weak, soft spoken victim. Nothing could be further from the truth.

Truth: *When He spoke it was with full authority and when He remained silent in front of His accusers, it was out of wisdom and strength, not fear or weakness. Never forget He had the power to zap every one of his enemies, yet chose grace and mercy to the point of death. This is a demonstration of supernatural strength we can never understand. When His Father's house was being abused, He got angry. He made a whip and He used force. And He never sinned. (John 2:12-17)*

This week's lesson will be draining so I am keeping it short. Leave space in this week if possible. It's important not to fill up your week with activities when you are dealing with a lot of anger.

Make time to do something just for you this week.

Write an anger letter to your husband (he never has to see it). This is for you. It's important to say goodbye to the man you thought you were married to and let out some of the anger. For some this will be easy as your pen flies over the page and cuss words flow. For others, you will want to focus on God's grace and your husband's redemption, but I want you to tap into the anger that is there. It's a natural human response to be angry when lied to and betrayed. It may not be pretty or Godly, but its human. *(By the way, not all anger is sin. Christ got angry at the Pharisees often.)* It's important to feel in order to heal! *(Use as many pages as needed.)*

Answer the journal prompt on the bottom of page 90 in *Hope After Betrayal.*

_____

_____

_____

_____

Write one thing you learned about your anger this week.

_____

_____

_____

_____

Lesson Six - Shadowlands

✎ Homework ✎

Read Chapter Six, pages 92-103 in *Hope After Betrayal*.

Pride is the root of all sin. It tells us in one form or another we are the god of our situation. There is a capital *"I"* in this word. Because what I want is at the center. Even when I am feeling less than or like I am putting others first, under the surface often lurks some benefit or focus on me. These shadowlands will surround us until we go home to be with the Lord. Its part of being fallen and having flesh that battles for preeminence.

The best we can do is seek God's perspective and wisdom, keeping Him on the throne. He can then show us that which we will never see on our own.

Humility is the other side of this coin. It is the byproduct of surrendering my self-sufficiency to the Lord and leaning on His understanding alone. It is evidence the Holy Spirit is in control. A friend said to me, *"If you have to say you are humble, or humbly doing something, then it's not true humility."* This struck me as harsh, but then I realized she was right. Much like my pride which operates outside of my peripheral vision, humility is the same. Others will smell its sweet aroma though I am unaware. I pray for the Lord to cultivate this in my life as I keep my eyes on Him instead of trying to be humble in my own strength. Do you see the irony?

Can you think of someone who is humble? Is there someone in your life or a character from a movie or show who exemplifies humility? What does it look like?

_____

_____

_____

_____

_____

In the book *Hope After Betrayal*, I talk about some of the shovels we dig our tunnels of pride with. List some of the shovels you use.

_____

_____

_____

_____

_____

_____

With the above shovels in mind, can you write your own lie?

Lie # 12: _____

_____

_____

_____

_____

_____

_____

_____

Now use your Bible and write your own truth from His Word.

Truth: _____

_____

_____

_____

_____

Pray about who you could ask to point out a blind spot. It needs to be someone you trust who has known you for a while. Write about what they say; try not to respond right away. If it stings, there is most likely some truth to work through.

_____

_____

_____

_____

Find your own *"Path Light."* Search scripture until God brings you to the promise He has for you. Write it down and put it where you can see it. Claim it for yourself each time you read it!

_____

_____

_____

_____

_____

_____

Answer the journal prompt on the bottom of page 103 in *Hope After Betrayal.*

_____

_____

_____

_____

_____

_____

_____

_____

_____

Lesson Seven - Glowworms

✎ Homework ✎

Read Chapter Seven, pages 104-112 in *Hope After Betrayal*.

Beautiful, mysterious, amazing grace — you are counter to human nature yet you elevate it. To some, grace feels like weakness, but to those who have paid the price to offer grace we know it takes strength beyond our own. Much like the gift of friendship, when someone says, *"I choose you,"* it warms the heart. But God's favor, that you could never earn, is the ultimate gift and the pinnacle of being wanted and loved by the One who created you. It's a wonder that every person isn't clamoring for this gift.

Even those of us who have accepted Christ often struggle to fully receive His gift of grace. It feels too easy at times when the enemy would offer the whip to punish ourselves. Conversely, it feels too hard when we want to retain the right to punish someone who has hurt us. There is an innate need to see justice done and grace feels contradictory. Justice belongs to God; we must throw away the human scales.

Step one is to remember why we need a Savior. Our sin cries out for blood, yet was paid for by Christ. Once we really see how dark our hearts are, the only thing to do is fall down before the Lord and give praise for the grace that offers life instead of the death we deserve. Once we accept this gift of Grace, the only choice is to offer it to others. Step two is to let go of your scales, levels, or comparisons and stand firmly on the level ground at the foot of the cross. We must trust God's justice even though it may not look accurate or potent in the moment. We must cling to grace as the life raft it is and then offer a seat to those in our life.

So many songs have been written on this topic. Spend some time listening to worship music and let the truth of grace wash over you, fill you, and bring freedom from self-condemnation or selfish condemnation.

Read Psalm 113 and then write out your own psalm of praise.

_____

_____

_____

_____

Lie #13: As Christians we should see true justice done on earth.

I assumed the Lord would have my back, but I forgot I live in a broken world incapable of true justice. And my measure of what is just is also broken.

Truth: Only God can judge because He sees inside every heart. *Don't pick on people, jump on their failures, criticize their faults—unless, of course, you want the same treatment. That critical spirit has a way of boomeranging. It's easy to see a smudge on your neighbor's face and be oblivious to the ugly sneer on your own.* (Matthew 7:1-2)

We will see justice but it may not be until we are home with the Lord.

I am only responsible for me and my heart before the Lord. I must learn to stop comparing or judging another person's righteousness and focus on my own.

What aspect of grace is the most difficult for you?

_____

_____

_____

_____

_____

_____

Become aware of the negative messages in your mind. Write them down and take time to find a scripture that deflects the lie or negative attitude.

_____

_____

_____

_____

_____

Read the *"Path Lights"* beginning on page 111 in *Hope After Betrayal.* Find your own *"Path Light."* Search scripture until God brings you to the promise He has for you. Write it down and put it where you can see it. Claim it for yourself each time you read it!

_____

_____

_____

_____

_____

Answer the journal prompt on the bottom of page 112 in *Hope After Betrayal.*

_____

_____

_____

_____

_____

Lesson Eight - Firefly

✎ Homework ✎

Read Chapter Eight, pages 113-120 in *Hope After Betrayal*.

This chapter is one of the most powerful if you let God make a way for His forgiveness to flow through you unobstructed by pride. I believe true forgiveness can only come through His power. I have found the harder I try, the more difficult this kind of release is. Only when I confess that my injury is too big and painful for me to let go of, can the Spirit of God move in my heart. Forgiveness = freedom! I pray you feel light and are able to soar after this week! Grace offers a bridge to others regardless of whether they help build it or pay the toll. Forgiveness counts every penny of the unpaid tolls and says, *"I've got it."* Before I understood this concept, I would let others cross the bridge, wave an *"I forgive you"* banner and fill my pockets with resentments — my reward for being so *"spiritual."* But I was not a bridge, I was simply a doormat. Forgiveness doesn't ignore the cost or pretend it isn't there. On the contrary, every coin had to be counted and the loss felt. Only then could I ask God to help me pay the cost and deal with my heart regardless of whether or not the other person knew or was appreciative. The work of forgiveness is primarily between me and God, having little to do with the person I forgive. They may not even be around or alive.

Go through this chapter again and fill the two columns regarding forgiveness.

What forgiveness is...

_____

_____

_____

_____

_____

_____

_____

_____

What forgiveness is not…

_____

_____

_____

_____

_____

_____

Lie #14 Forgiveness is weakness; it's better to stand firmly against an affront.

This feels true when the betrayal and pain runs deep. Letting go can feel like giving in. There are times when righteous anger is appropriate, but unforgiveness never is.

Truth: Forgiveness and grace are the great riches the Lord offers and requires we share. Then others will see and know He is real. When we offer forgiveness where the world would not, we shine the light of His glory and affirm the same forgiveness we have received. True forgiveness is a work of God in us. *In him we have redemption through his blood, the forgiveness of sins, in accordance with the riches of God's grace.* (Ephesians 1:7)

Have you made note of those you still may need to forgive? Consider the ways you have fallen short. Ask God to give you a glimpse into your own heart. Whether you feel too far gone for God's forgiveness or you have no major *"sin markers,"* look at your motivations and desires in the light of the One who sees it all and knows it all. Agree with Him about it and then look into His loving face.

Now, put a mark on the line that represents where you are on the *"Forgiven"* line. You see, we can't offer to others what we have not fully received ourselves.

Low_____|_____|_____High

Don't believe | Willing to be clean | Praising the Lord for
that which I could
never earn!

Think about where you are with your spouse and anyone else who has injured you.

Plot where you feel you are on the forgiveness scale.

Low_____|_____|_____High

Not ready   Willing to begin   Looking to the Lord!

Take a minute to pray. Ask the Lord what the next step is. Take time to listen. Praise Him for His care and patience. Write out your thoughts.

_____

_____

_____

_____

_____

_____

_____

_____

_____

_____

_____

_____

What aspect of forgiveness still holds you back?

_____

_____

_____

_____

_____

_____

Where are you on the trust continuum?

Low_____|_____|_____High

Not ready | Hopeful yet cautious | Taking steps

List some of your spouse's behaviors that still cause concern
and what you need to see to begin to trust.

_____

_____

_____

_____

_____

_____

_____

_____

Lesson Nine - Prisms

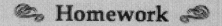 Homework

Read Chapter Nine, pages 122-131 in *Hope After Betrayal.*

Oh woman, you are beautiful inside and out! *(Luke 1:28)* Your heavenly Father knit you together in your mother's womb. *(Psalm 139:13)* He counts every hair on your head *(Matthew 10:30)* and saves every tear. *(Psalm 56:8)* He sings over you with unfathomable tenderness. *(Zephaniah 3:17)* He is all you need. Hold onto these truths precious one. Know your worth by knowing how great the One is who crafted you unique— one of a kind.

There is so much I could write on this topic for I wasted so many tears on the lies that would say otherwise. Today, when I stand before a mirror or look at an unflattering picture, and hear the destroyer whisper something derogatory, I pray His Word. I say to myself, *"I am fearfully and wonderfully made."* It's a great silencer of the internal critic.

As for those tears, I used to hate them. One day I heard a speaker say there are those who pray for the "gift of tears." It struck me that they are a gift. When I see a rainbow I think, the light would not be able to display its beauty if the clouds were impenetrable brick walls. To cry honestly before the Lord is to be transparent. To be transparent enables the light to shine through. There is no better place for the Lord's glory to be seen than through our weakness.

Lie #15 God uses those who are smart, attractive, and _____. (fill in the blank)

Truth: The enemy's role is to kill and destroy. He can't create; he can only distort or destroy. So when you feel less than, feel the barb from a critical word, or feel put down, recognize the author of dark places and put it before the Light of Truth. The world is fickle, but God is faithful. Ask Him to show you how He can use that very flaw you try to hide. Remember, when you are transparent you give others permission to be too.

Lie #16 Adding or changing _____

would make my life better or easier. *(fill in the blank)*

Truth: It's easy to point to some *"thing"* or circumstance and say this is the one thing that brings me down. Don't fall into this pit for when you fix that one thing you will find there is just one more. Until we can be like Paul in Philippians 4:12, content in any circumstance or situation we find ourselves in, there will be no peace. Yet in Christ there is peace far beyond our circumstance.

Take some time to read the Psalms. Jot down any verses that ring true or strike a chord. Choose one to memorize. It's the best weapon we have to combat the lies of the evil one.

Psalm _____

_____

_____

_____

_____

Psalm _____

_____

_____

_____

_____

Psalm _____

_____

_____

_____

_____

Psalm _____

_____

_____

_____

_____

Make a list here of your five best qualities, internal and external. Invite those you trust to help you with this list. There is a good chance they see things you don't! Consider it a treasure hunt! Don't move on until you complete this list!

_____

_____

_____

_____

_____

I am inviting you to engage further with the Word and make these questions your own. I challenge you to seek for the truth you need today. This book called the Bible is truly amazing. It's alive with whatever you need and pours out the heart of God with every love letter written thousands of years ago, yet still relevant today!

Open your mouth and taste, open your eyes and see— how good God is. Blessed are you who run to him. (Psalm 34:8)

Lesson Ten - Path Lights

✎ Homework ✎

Read Chapter Ten, pages 133-140 in *Hope After Betrayal.*

There will be another bend in the road. It's all part of living in a broken world and in the arena of truth. I have learned it's much safer to prepare for the worst and hope for the best. I heard a pastor once say, *"Everyone is either going into, coming out of, or in the middle of a crisis."* I didn't like it, but time has proven just how true he was. I can't control the crisis, but I can choose how to respond. I can be discouraged or I can lean into whatever comes, trusting the One who holds me in His righteous right hand. I couldn't see the power of this choice until I stopped trying to control or take responsibility for things that were not mine.

Before we can move forward it's important to take a hard look at your situation, and invite the Lord into the most difficult parts. He loves a challenge and is still in the miracle business. Don't doubt it for a moment. I could fill another book with all the ways I have seen Him meet the needs of His kids!

Earlier, I mentioned planning for the worst and hoping for the best. I will ask you to take some time this week and prayerfully consider making a plan. Don't draw a map or a hard line because God needs to guide, but use the mind He gave you and wise counsel He provides to really sift between what is real and what are the dreams you have. What are the choices you can control and those that belong to someone else. Give God your dreams, the future you would paint, then deal with the real—actual—truth.

Make a plan for the *"worst case scenario"* given where you and your husband are now. Consider where you could both go and the poor choices he could still make. It's important not to let this take you down a dark path of fear. If you can't be objective get some help with this exercise. Try to stand on the outside & look in.

Prayerfully, consider the practical plans you need to put in place. Imagine how you would counsel your best friend. Don't obsess about the negative and get stuck in believing it's only a matter of time before it all falls apart. That is not helpful. Instead, take a quick look at the potential in order to make your plan before the crisis makes sense. Worry is not the goal. You will find peace in knowing that IF the worst happens you are prepared. Don't forget the *"hope for the best"* part. Write out the plans you need to make regarding the following:

*Work*_____

_____

_____

_____

_____

*Finances*_____

_____

_____

_____

_____

*Kids / Childcare*_____

_____

_____

_____

_____

*Self Care*_____

_____

_____

_____

*Other*_____

_____

_____

_____

_____

You may not have all the answers, so write down people you may need to meet with: family, pastor, counselor, career counselor, lawyer, etc. Pray for the Lord to lead this process and then listen and watch for His handprint. Remember, you may not need this but it is important to see yourself as independent and complete in Christ.

Journal about this process — write down any questions for your leader.

_____

_____

_____

_____

_____

_____

Lesson 11 - What's Next?

✎ Homework ✎

Read Chapter Eleven, pages 141-151 in *Hope After Betrayal*.

This chapter most likely has already been read since most of my friends confessed to reading it first. I understand because my story begs the question, *"How does your husband feel?"* I am blessed because my husband chooses daily to seek God for his future and choices. I thank him all the time for his willingness to let God tear out his heart and do an overhaul. It has been hard to watch at times, but to this day he is my hero and the bravest man I know.

With that said, there are so many women whose husbands refuse to give up their lies. For whatever reason, the work feels too hard. This leaves their wives with two choices. Ironically, they are the same two choices I had.

1. I will move forward into my unknown journey trusting the Lord's love and purpose for me.

2. I will surrender to the pain and settle into the rut of complacency and victimhood.

When you see them written out, you might think, *"Duh, who would choose #2?"* But it's more about refusing to choose; it's more subtle and many women land here. The enemy convinces them they got a raw deal even from God, or they believe they don't deserve any better, or any number of lies that feel true to a broken spirit.

Now those who are facing or have experienced divorce may scoff at this and say to me, *"You don't understand Meg, your husband chose to change."* The truth is, I too had to wrestle with the reality that I would live with a man who any day could make a poor choice that could devastate me. I had to come to the place, before I knew the outcome, where I knew beyond a shadow of a doubt that should that day come, and the Lord freed me to leave — I would be okay. I had everything I needed in my Lord: Provider, Bridegroom, and the Lover of my soul!

But don't take my word for it. Hear it from a woman who has walked this path:

"My world as I knew it came to a screeching halt when my husband of 20 years got caught in his secret sexual addiction. I felt shocked, horrified and so confused. Several days later, he and I sat with a local pastor who asked many questions and carefully observed the situation. He spent four hours with us and shared his concerns. I was hurt and angry. I wished my husband would go away, disappear, or die. That felt way easier than dealing with what I was having to accept as my new normal.

The pastor told us we were a family in crisis and he was not sure that our marriage would survive the betrayal. He proceeded to tell us both what we each needed to do to begin the healing process. He shared with me that I had three choices: 1) divorce 2) denial, which would lead to divorce or 3) work on myself, my healing, my issues — not the marriage.

I made the decision that day to commit to working on myself. I started attending a class for women whose partners had sexual addiction (SA). I needed to understand what it was, how it had affected us both. I needed to know how this could have been happening without me knowing. I began hearing words that I had never really heard of or understood — codependency, co-addict, etc. I cried as other women shared their stories of disclosures and discoveries.

Had I really been living in a "church bubble" for so long that I was that naive to what so many Christian men struggled with? I felt overwhelmed with the need for classes, support and counseling for myself. And what about my three kids? What help did they need? I had days where I felt like I could not do it anymore. And I wanted to run. But I knew I had to heal and recover so that I could help my kids do the same.

Within a year, I was blessed to find a support group for the partners of men struggling with SA. It was an amazing place of healing to know I was not alone. We began learning together from books like, _Boundaries_, _Changes That Heal_, _Safe People_ and _Hiding From Love_ as a group. I began to grow and dig deep into my issues and my past wounding. The healthier I got, the more work I did to change, the less my husband did. After three separations, we were divorced four years after disclosure.

It took a loving community supporting me, a great counselor and a lot of truth from those I trusted, for me to finally realize that he was not going to do his recovery. I was free to make the choice to walk down a different path —one towards emotional wholeness. He was free to make his choice, and he said no to the path of health.

Divorce was one of the hardest but best choices I ever made. Investing in my healing, choosing to grow as a woman and a mother has helped my kids to heal. It has been a process for all of us to move forward, grieve the losses and allow God to restore our hearts."

~Marietta~

I pray this workbook has been helpful and that you are already feeling the benefits of doing your own personal work. Now, it's time to decide what your next step is. The journey to wholeness is a lifelong road. Pray about where the Lord would guide you next: whether individual counseling, support group, Bible study, etc. Write out your decision and then tell a safe friend who will hold you accountable to follow through.

This work we do will pay dividends in our life, and the lives of those we love for eternity!

Note from author:

Thank you for using this material and for staying with it. I would love to hear from you. So consider going to our website at hopeafterbetrayal.com and sending your thoughts about your journey, or you can post a comment on our Facebook page.

Hope & Healing,

Meg

Hope In A Box

Everything You Need To Start Your Own Healing Heart Group

This turn-key curriculum contains over $380 worth of tools to help you lead women from hurt and devastation to hope and healing.

For more information go to:

http://www.hopeafterbetrayal.com/product/hope-in-a-box-curriculum/

A Devotional Journal
for anyone suffering loss

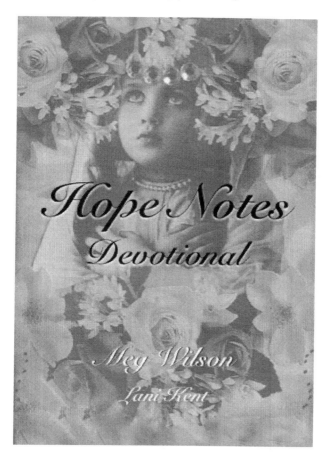

Hope Notes gently walks the reader through the six stages of grief. Twenty Scriptures in Shock, Denial, Anger, Bargaining, Sadness, and Acceptance encourages the healing process and allows for an individual pace. Each stage is beautifully enhanced with an image by Lani Kent, therapeutic artist. Finally, there is a gift worthy book for the brokenhearted.

(not specific to sexual addiction)
Available at www.hopeafterbetrayal.com/our-materials/

Proceeds from the sale of this book go to

which offers hope and healing to women
devastated by their husband's sexual
brokenness. For more information or to
order additional books, go to
www.hopeafterbetrayal.com

Made in the USA
Middletown, DE
17 April 2018